The Martin Brothers

by David L. Biehl

PRAIRIE MUSE PLATINUM

www.prairiemuse.com

Dedication

I would like to dedicate this book to my good friend Fred A. Bosselman who got this whole project started when he asked me one day, "Do you know the story of the Martin Brothers, and would you be interested in sculpting a life-sized Bronze of the incident?"

That request started me on a quest to find out all I could about the Martin family, and it afforded me my first opportunity to create a life-sized monument and write their story.

This book and the bronze sculpture entitled "A Narrow Escape" are permanent reminders of a great story in Nebraska History and the conflict between two very different cultures that led to political tension and ethnic violence between the indigenous Native American Indian and the early Pioneers of The Great Plains.

> We live under the sky we do not own
> We drink from the well we did not dig
> We prosper from the furrow we did not turn
> We inhabit the land our forefathers fought for
> >   Now
> We are the stewards of this land that was given
>
> - unknown

NARROW ESCAPE

The Sculpture on the front cover entitled "A Narrow Escape" was commissioned by Fred A. Bosselman and Sculpted by David L. Biehl in 2011.

One of these sculptures now stands in front of the Gus Fonner Rotunda at Stuhr Musem in Grand Island, Nebraska, and a second one was placed in front of the Hastings Museum in July of 2013. The sculpture is approximately 10 feet long and 7 feet tall.

THE SCULPTOR

I grew up on a farm just northwest of Lexington, Nebraska, and from the time I was very little I was involved with horses, cattle and farming. I guess it was these experiences that set me on a path to become a Veterinarian. To become a Vet I studied all of the sciences without much thought of art and its craft. But in 2003 I attended a large bronze art show in Loveland, Colorado and I liked what I saw. I thought to myself, I think I would like to try that. So with the encouragement of my wife Cindy, I purchased some clay and I taught myself to sculpt.

I think having a background in anatomy has helped me transition from someone who works on horses to one who can create them in bronze…I find people to be a little more difficult.

For me it will always be a hobby. I tell people "I play with clay". I sculpt because I like to, and I have found it to be extremely relaxing and rewarding.

Foreword

There have been several accounts published that tell the story of the Martin Brothers' encounter with a Native American war party along the Platte River west of Doniphan, Nebraska. In this writing, every effort has been made to sort through the many retellings and glean the most likely record of events that bring to light this true and harrowing story.

MAP 1 - THE GREAT PLAINS

CHAPTER 1

The Great Plains

The story of the Martin Family takes place in an area known as the Great Plains (SEE MAP 1). Before we get to the Martin Family and their settling in the vast prairie, it's important that we understand the history of the area.

The Great Plains was a broad expanse of land extending west of the Missouri and Mississippi rivers to the foothills of the Rockies, south to the Mexican border and north to Canada. The first people to inhabit the Great Plains were Paleo-Indians who crossed over to North America via the Bering Straits land bridge.

The Bering Straits was a strip of land and ice between eastern Siberia in Russia and the present day Alaska. (SEE MAP 2). It is not known exactly when the Paleo-Indians came to America, but historians believe it could have been between seventeen and twenty-five thousand years ago. It took thousands of years, but eventually about ten to twelve thousand years ago these nomadic people were thriving in what we now call the Great Plains.

Over these many thousands of years, several different tribes evolved, each carving out their own way of life. Two of the tribes relative to this story were the Sioux and the Pawnee.

The Sioux nation was one of the most affluent of the

tribes in the western Great Plains. Its people roamed the land from the lakes and forests of Minnesota across the plains of North and South Dakota and west to the mountains of Wyoming and south to western Nebraska.

Within the Sioux Nation there were many different bands and tribes. The Brule and Ogallala were two of the Sioux tribes that traveled to Nebraska. They claimed western and central Nebraska as their territory and hunting grounds. These tribes were fierce groups and often had conflicts with other Indian tribes or intruders. In the spring and summer they relied on the Platte and Republican River valleys to hunt buffalo and other smaller game. In the fall they migrated back north to the area of the Black Hills where they could find abundant fuel and shelter to better survive the winter.

The other Indian Nation that pertains to our story was the Pawnee. Historically, the Pawnee were not a fighting tribe and had resigned themselves to getting along with other tribes and early settlers. They lived in permanent earth lodges where they primarily farmed and hunted the surrounding plains but did not travel long distances to hunt. Their large rounded earth lodges were built over a shallow excavated floor, framed with poles, then covered with smaller poles and thatch. One such earthen lodge is on permanent display at Stuhr Museum in Grand Island, Nebraska.

The Pawnee stayed in central Nebraska most of the year, traveling to the Platte and Republican River valleys to hunt buffalo in the spring.

So, for about ten thousand years, the Native American Indians lived and thrived on the Great Plains. Each Indian nation and tribe developed their own individual identity and customs. It's startling to note, then, that it would take only three hundred years after the first exposure to European explorers for the Native Americans to have their land taken and their whole way of life destroyed.

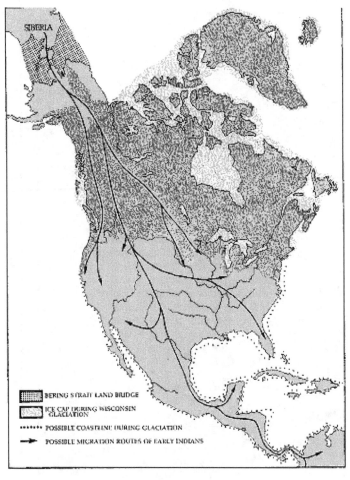

MAP 2 - THE BERING STRAIT LAND BRIDGE AND THE MIGRATION OF EARLY INDIANS

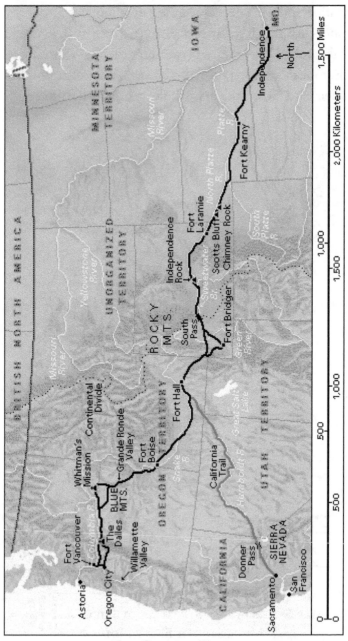

THE OREGON TRAIL

CHAPTER 2

Indians Encounter Europeans

The plains Indians were first exposed to Europeans when Francisco de Coronado, a Spanish Conquistador, arrived on the high plains prairie. This first recorded meeting occurred in the Texas-Oklahoma area in the year 1540. Soon after that, the Spanish explorers moved as far north as Nebraska. Over the next two hundred and fifty years, opening of the fur and hide trade brought thousands of trappers and explorers of many ethnic cultures to the high plains. Fur trappers came from France, Spain, Britain, Russia and new Eastern America. This sporadic exploration of the area primarily followed the rivers because it was easier to bring supplies and take furs back by canoe than by ground transportation.

In 1802, under the leadership of President Thomas Jefferson, the United States bought the great expanse of land known as the Great Plains from France. This was the famous Louisiana Purchase. President Jefferson ordered Meriwether Lewis and William Clark to explore and map the area to find an easy passage to the Pacific Ocean.

From 1804 to 1806 Lewis and Clark traversed the area from the Missouri River to the west coast. They traveled the **Northern part** of the Great Plains and found a way, but it could not be traveled by wagons and made moving large amounts of freight unfeasible. With information and maps provided by the Lewis and Clark Expedition, a few hardy adventurers managed to migrate west—but they had to travel by canoe, horseback and pack mules.

President Jefferson—in order to find a better and easier way to the west coast—also ordered military exploration of the **Southern Great Plains**. In the summer of 1806, Jefferson commissioned Lt. Zebulon Pike to lead a military expedition west from near St. Louis, Missouri. He met up with the Republican River Pawnees in an area between the current towns of Guide Rock and Red Cloud, Nebraska. With the help of the Pawnee, he continued southwest, following old Indian trails and the Republican River Valley of Southern Nebraska. As their journey progressed, they headed south across the prairie for the Arkansas River, following it upstream until Pike's journey was blocked by the Royal Gorge and the Rocky Mountains. Again, no easily accessible route to the far west was established.

Soon after, explorers taking a more **Central Great Plains** route followed the Platte River where it joins to the Missouri River, traveling west and continuing up the north branch of the Platte River where it splits from the main river at North Platte, Nebraska. (SEE MAP 3)

The explorers continued along the North Platte and found South Pass, which is a thirty-five mile saddle-shaped pass over the Continental Divide in Wyoming. From South Pass the group continued on to Oregon. They had found a feasible trail suitable for wagon travel. This trail would later be called the California-Oregon Trail.

With discovery of an easier route to the areas along the west coast, thousands of homesteading pioneers were allowed the chance to seek their fortunes.

Changes were beginning to come faster to the wide open prairie with the discovery of the Platte River route. Mountain-men, missionaries and traders led the way by using the Platte River valley in order to survive the dry, harsh Great Plains weather. The valley also offered a somewhat level terrain.

As more settlers began to use the trail, it became not a single path but rather a multitude of paths as wide as a mile in some places. Although it began as an unconnected series of trails used by the Native American Indians, fur traders expanded the route to transport pelts to trading posts and rendezvous points. It eventually became the major route across the plains.

Joel Walker is credited as the first settler to make the complete two thousand mile journey from east to west in 1840. Large scale migration really got started in 1843 when a wagon train of over eight hundred people with one hundred twenty wagons and over five thousand head of cattle made the five month trip from St. Joseph, Missouri to the west coast.

From 1846 to 1868, Mormons escaping religious persecution headed toward Salt Lake and followed parts of the Oregon Trail. They started across the plains from Council Bluffs, Iowa and traveled along the north bank of the Platte River to avoid the heavier traffic on the Oregon Trail along the south bank. The Mormon Trail eventually joined the Oregon Trail in Wyoming at Fort Bridger.

Many pioneers departed the heavily used portion of

the trail to avoid the muddy ruts of previous wagons and to find suitable grass for grazing their livestock.

The route had its difficulties. In the spring, creeks and rivers would flood making crossing with heavy wagons and teams difficult. In the summer, the tremendous heat and sudden thunder and hail storms caused occasional havoc.

The number of travelers using the Oregon Trial exploded with the discovery of gold at Sutter's Mill in California in 1848. Later, in 1858, gold was discovered in the Denver and Boulder, Colorado areas. As many as 400,000 immigrants associated with the gold rushes in California and Colorado used the Oregon Trail to try to gain their fortune.

During this time there were large numbers of people traveling through the Great Plains, and for the most part they did just that—traveled through. Few of these travelers stayed in the Nebraska territory. It would be another decade before settlers came to Nebraska and stayed. In fact it would take an act of Congress called the Homestead Act to convince new Americans and immigrants to travel and stay in the Central Great Plains.

With the massive numbers of Europeans and Euro-Americans arriving in the area, two distinct catastrophes would impact the Great Plains native people. The first catastrophe was the spreading of diseases that the Americans and Europeans brought with them. The Native American Indian had no natural resistance to Small Pox and Cholera, and thousands would perish from these diseases.

The second catastrophe was the zealous hunting and

trapping by the new arrivals. Their modern weaponry killed large numbers of wildlife and buffalo. This was significant because of the tremendous changes it brought to the hunting grounds the natives relied upon to live. As the number of Americans and Europeans arriving to the area grew, the well-being and natural way of life of the Native American was being severely challenged.

DID YOU KNOW?

The Oregon Trail—sometimes called the Oregon-California Trail—migration is one of the most important events in American history. The Oregon Trail was a 2,170-mile route from the Missouri River to the west coast. It was the only feasible land route for settlers to get to the coast. From 1843 until 1869 when the first transcontinental railroad was completed there were over 500,000 people who made the trip in covered wagons pulled by mules, horses, or oxen. The trip usually took 4 to 6 months by wagon traveling 15 miles a day.

The only other way to get to the west coast was by sea and that could take almost a year. However, the trip across the open plains was not without peril. If they left Missouri too early in the spring, there was not enough grass for grazing and creeks and rivers were often more difficult to cross because of high water. If they left too late, they would get caught by the winter snows in the South Pass through the Rockies.

Another problem for the travelers was Cholera and Small Pox. Some wagon trains lost two-thirds of their party. Bodies were left on the side of the trail or buried in shallow graves that animals would dig up scattering human bones and skulls along the trail. The Oregon Trail was sometimes called the "longest graveyard in America."

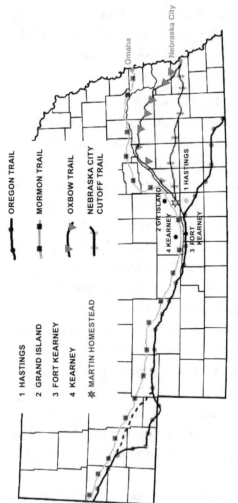

Did You Know? Nebraska is known as the "Historic Trails State". The Lewis and Clark, Mormon, Pioneer, Pony Express, Oregon and California Trails all cross Nebraska along with many lesser known trails like the Nebraska City Cut-Off, the Oxbow, Texas Ogallala Cattle Trail and the Overland Trail.

Map: Location of the Martin Homestead and the Historic Trails of Nebraska

CHAPTER 3

The Homestead Act Effect

The first Homestead Act had been proposed by northern Republicans before the Civil War in 1859, but had been blocked in Congress by Southern Democrats who wanted the lands open for settlement by slave-owners. After the southern states seceded from the Union in 1861, Abraham Lincoln—the newly elected 16th president—and the Republican Party passed the long delayed bill in 1862.

This Homestead Act of 1862 had few requirements. The "Homesteader" had to be the head of the household or at least 21 years old and have never raised arms against the Union. They had to live on the designated 160 acre land claim, build a home, make improvements and cultivate and raise a crop for a minimum of five years. It allowed immigrants (not U.S. citizens), farmers without their own land, single women and former slaves to homestead. The qualification of never having raised arms against the Union kept seceding Southerners from applying. The Homestead Act had both positive and negative effects.

The positive effects of the Homestead Act gave a vast number of people of lesser means a chance to get ahead. It brought thousands of people to the west and small towns and villages began to develop where there had been nothing before but open prairie. In Abraham Lincoln's view, it also lessened the chances that rich land-owning slave owners of the South could take all the land for themselves. This was something he was concerned about if the North was to lose the Civil War.

President Lincoln's Homestead Act of 1862 also had many negative effects. The impact the "Homesteader" had on the indigenous Native America Indians was completely devastating. The land that was previously theirs to hunt and live on was being taken and redistributed by the U.S. Government. The government, in order to free up the land for the settlers, opted to round up the natives like cattle. The Indians were forced to give up their free lifestyles and move to reservations in an effort to make them more manageable.

With this onslaught of land grabbing by thousands of homesteaders, the land was unable to sustain its natural wildlife. The buffalo herds that the Native Americans depended on for thousands of years for survival were disappearing. Some of the Indian tribes did cooperate with the government while others did not. A few of the more dominant hostile tribes decided that it was time to make a stand and defend their land and customs. To do this, the Sioux tribes of South Dakota and western Nebraska decided to make a last ditch attempt to take their spring hunting grounds along the Platte River back from the newly arriving settlers.

CHAPTER 4

The Martin Family Begins

George Martin married Ann Weavers, a widow with a young son, George, and a daughter, Eliza, in Wallington County, England. They spent the next several years in Yorkshire, England where George senior was a horse trainer for a stable. They were blessed with a daughter, Hepzibah and a son, Henry Nathaniel.

In 1851 they came to the United States and spent a brief period in Cleveland, Ohio where another son was born, Robert Ower. Soon after, they moved to Henry County Illinois where George farmed for nine years. During this time, two more children were born, a son, Willie, and a daughter, Annie.

In 1859 the Martins sold their farm in Illinois with the thought of moving west. With that in mind, George, Ann and their six children moved to Fremont County Iowa, just across the Missouri River from the present day Nebraska City, Nebraska. By this time, Ann's first son and George's step-son, George Weaver, was an adult and stayed behind, enlisting in the Union Army and later fought in the Civil War.

Nebraska City had become a starting point for travelers heading west and was especially known for the large amount of freight that left there and headed west to supply military forts, gold miners in the Rockies and small settlements springing up all along the Oregon Trail.

The Nebraska City Cutoff was a shorter and quicker way to head west. It joined the Oregon Trail at Fort Kearney. (SEE MAP)

It was as a "bull-whacker", the man that drove the oxen for the freighter wagons, that George Martin got his first exposure to the central Great Plains. The "bull-whacker" walked along with the teams of oxen with a long whip and kept the cattle moving at a steady pace and in the correct direction.

George made several trips with the Freighter trains and fell in love with the Platte River valley. It has been estimated that in 1864 twenty three million pounds of freight left the banks of the Missouri River at Nebraska City and was hauled westward by 2,132 wagons pulled by four to six oxen each. These numbers take into consideration that each wagon and team of oxen made the trip back and forth three to four times a year.

The country was yet unsettled, but the ground was level and fertile and most importantly, water could be found only a few feet below the surface of the ground. The Platte also offered adequate surface water and wildlife for food and hides.

The area George was interested in was along the Nebraska City Cut-off twenty-five miles east of Fort Kearney. George told Ann about the layout and nature of the land and they both decided that they would try to move there someday. That day soon came with the passage of the Homestead Act of 1862.

CHAPTER 5

More Than a Home

Ann Martin was more than just physically tough, as later accounts will attest. She also had deep values and principles that followed her Christian faith. She agreed to move her family to the wild frontier, but with one condition. She did not want her home to be near the trail, so as not to expose her children to the riff-raff and crudeness of the freighters.

George, on the other hand, having worked and traveled on the trail several times, thought being along the trail had great business potential and he had a spot all picked out. As it turned out he was right. George made an agreement with Ben Holiday, owner of the Western Stage Company, and agreed to build one of the rest stops along the stage coach route. In June of 1862, with a wagon load of supplies, George headed west from Nebraska City with his three sons; Nathaniel, thirteen; Robert, eleven and Willie, who was only eight. It took them seven days, but they finally arrived at a location approximately 8 miles west of the current Doniphan, Nebraska.

The spot that George had picked out from his travels with the Freighters was about a mile south of the Platte River. George decided the first thing they needed to do was dig a well. The digging was easy in the sandy soil and within a few feet down their hole began to fill with water. To keep the hole from filling in with sand and dirt, George Martin took a wooden barrel from the wagon they had used to haul water, knocked out the bottom and the top and placed it in the hole. After pulling a few buckets of cloudy water from the newly dug well, it began to clear. Within a few minutes they had a source of clean, drinkable water.

After the well was dug, George Martin needed a house for his family. As did most of the pioneers of this time, they used what was available. Sod was plentiful and a two room sod house was built. The back room was for the family and the front room would be for guests of the stage line or other travelers seeking shelter for the night. After a few weeks of intense labor, the Martin boys finished building a home suitable for the rest of the family and in late September of 1862, George brought Ann and the rest of the children to live on the prairie. There is no account of Ann's thoughts or comments when she found out her house was built next to the Nebraska City Cutoff trail.

By this time fall was approaching, and a small sod barn and corral were built from cottonwood timber gathered along the banks and river islands along the Platte. Additional wood was used to shore-up the sides of the well for easier access. They were set for winter with a well, a new sod house and barn.

In the spring of 1863, the Martins planted their first crops. The three oldest boys—Nathaniel, Robert and Willie—transplanted a few cottonwood trees gathered from the river banks to provide shade around the homestead. Ann and Willie, who was now nine years old, took two wagons east to Nebraska City to get more supplies. They would make this trip five or six times a year. It was almost 290 miles round trip and it would take them five days to get to Nebraska City and six days to come back home. Coming back with loaded wagons always took an extra day. Ann and Willie would encounter many friendly native Pawnee Indians along the route and other settlers as well. After a time, they became friends with many of the settlers and Pawnee and would often stay with their friends along their journey.

CHAPTER 6

The Great Buffalo Hunt

George Martin had not gotten where he was in life without being adventurous. So when an opportunity arrived to try something new, he jumped at the chance.

In the spring of 1863, a pelt trader and hunter stopped at the Martin ranch to get a drink and buy some hay for his horses. He noticed George showing interest in one of his horses and remarked to George that he was a trained Buffalo Hunting horse. Before the trader left the Martin homestead, George and the trader made a deal. George was a lover of horses and now was a proud new owner of a highly trained Buffalo horse, or so he thought.

Not long after the purchase of his buffalo horse, word came of a large herd of buffalo just a day's travel to the southwest. George, without hesitation, gathered up two wagons and their only firearms. With his two rifles and a small pistol, George, Nathaniel (14) and Willie (9), along with the buffalo horse, headed southwest.

Along the way they stopped at a neighbor's place a few miles from their ranch. The man there was named Mabin and he had a small feed barn and Soddy dry goods store that he also called home. They told Mabin of the hunting trip and he elected to go along, adding another rifle and a mule to the hunting party.

The Martins and their friend continued onward to the place where the buffalo had been spotted. It didn't take long, for the next day the hunters found their prey. George quickly swung onto the unsaddled buffalo horse, clutching the rifle with the pistol tucked in his belt. Mabin and the two boys watched as George quietly rode toward the herd, circling out a lone buffalo for the kill.

It soon became obvious that the horse was reluctant, but George managed to get between the lone buffalo and the herd. The chosen buffalo ran for a short distance then whirled and faced the oncoming horse and rider. The irritated buffalo charged and the buffalo horse began to dart and weave. George, trying to stay atop his darting horse, lost the grip on his rifle and it tumbled to the ground.

By this time the buffalo was closing in on the rider and his horse. The horse—desperately trying to get away from the ill-tempered bison—dove sharply to the right and George landed on the ground. With the buffalo charging only a few feet away, George drew his pistol and with one lucky shot hit the rushing animal in the eye. The enraged buffalo spun round and round from the pain, giving George time to make a run for his horse. The elder Martin reached his horse that had been standing 40 to 50 yards away, but by this time the angered buffalo was in hot pursuit.

George had no time to swing on so he grasped the buffalo horse around his neck hanging on to the mane with all his strength. The horse bolted, kicking the enraged buffalo in the head, and then turned toward the wagons on a dead run with George dangling from his neck.

The injured beast was stunned from the kick in the head and it gave George and his horse time to escape to the waiting neighbor and two boys.

Mabin, naturally, began to taunt George by telling him he was a fool and that neither he nor his horse knew anything about hunting buffalo. Mabin surprised the Martins as he mounted his mule and headed toward the wounded animal, calling back over his shoulder, "this is how it's done."

His hunt was brutally short. The injured bison had gained his wits and quickly charged the oncoming mule and rider. The mule turned abruptly and Mabin, in an attempt to stay straddled on his steed, dropped his rifle. The pair came flying back to the wagons with the pursuing beast hooking the mule with his horns several times along the way.

Finally reaching the wagons, the three Martins and Mabin put the wagons between them and the angered buffalo. Both adult hunters had lost their rifles and seemed to be bewildered by the ordeal. The enraged buffalo, standing only a few yards away, pawed the ground to make another charge. Nat, without hesitation, took aim and dropped the charging beast just a few feet from the wagons with one fortunate shot.

Young Willie, who had stood by helplessly watching the wild and crazy proceedings, remarked later that night at the supper table that this was the most tender and sweet buffalo he had ever eaten.

It is unknown if this was the last buffalo hunt planned by George with the buffalo horse. No other hunting stories were documented.

CHAPTER 7

Pressure on the Prairie

Two years passed and the Martin family settled in, becoming comfortable with their newfound prairie life. They were some of the first settlers to the area and their closest neighbor was four miles away. The Martins were isolated, but were in constant contact with the Freighter bull-whackers, other homesteaders and people traveling with the stage line.

The local Pawnee Indians became good friends, and the Martin children would often play at the Indian encampments. It was a peaceful relationship. The Pawnee people often passed through the Platte Valley on trips between the Loup River in the north to the Republican River to the south where they hunted buffalo.

Buffalo were still present, but their numbers were beginning to dwindle. It soon became obvious that this area of the Great Plains was becoming more crowded with settlers and thus offered less area for Indians to hunt and live.

The local Pawnee tribes tried to live in peace with the settlers, but the Sioux and Cheyenne tribes from the northern areas were not so tolerant of the newcomers. After all, for thousands of years they had relied on the buffalo herds of the Republican and Platte Valleys to survive.

In the spring of 1864, the Sioux and Cheyenne tribes began to form small war parties and staged attacks along the South Platte River. It was a last ditch attempt to rid the area of settlers and take back the land.

The first recorded attack occurred near the current town of Julesburg, Colorado along the South Platte River branch. As the attacks moved slowly east, some settlers did pull up stakes and scurry back east across the Missouri River. Many traveled to Fort Kearney for protection.

While the Civil War was raging on in the eastern states, a smaller, lesser known war was being waged on the prairie of the Great Plains. A war that would last for about four years. Unfortunately for the warring Indian tribes, they had no idea that thousands of settlers were on their way to the area to claim their 160 acres of free land, and the Indian attempt to reclaim their land was futile.

The Martin family heard the horror stories of the Indian raids and massacres, but George and Ann were determined to stay. They had built up a nice ranch and business and decided they would take their chances.

One such attack—the Plum Creek Massacre— occurred on August 8, 1864 sixty miles west of the Martin home. That day, a hundred Sioux or Cheyenne or a combination of warring parties attacked a circle of wagons hauling freight westward toward Denver. Eleven members of the ox train were mortally wounded. Nancy Jane Morton, 19, was kidnapped along with a seven-year-old boy by the name of Danny Marble. Nancy Jane and Danny were later traded for and released. Nancy's recordings of her ordeal are written in the book, *Captive of the Cheyenne.*

Because of the unpleasant association of the attack with the village of Plum Creek, its name was changed to Lexington. Lexington is now located north and west of the site of the attack and massacre.

CHAPTER 8

Successful Business

Because of the location of the Martin Homestead along the trail and the fact that they were a stagecoach stop, George soon realized there was a big demand for hay, and thus, the opportunity to provide it. Freighter trains and settlers would stop at the Martin home to buy hay for their horses and oxen when grass for grazing was not in season on the prairie.

One hot summer day in August 1864, the two oldest boys, Henry Nathaniel, fifteen, and Robert Ower, twelve, were in the field putting up prairie grass hay with their father George. The three had been putting up hay and hauling it to their ranch for several days.

On this day in August they were loading hay on two wagons and were about two miles south of the house. Sunlight was beginning to fade and the cutting and loading of hay was complete for the day.

They were about to start for home when Nathaniel "Nat" noticed a small party of Indian braves west against the setting sun. The three were well aware of the stories of the Indian attacks on settlers to the west. Freighters had shared the rumors when they passed through the Martin homestead. They had heard of the raid on the wagon train at Plum Creek just a few days before.

George had the team of horses harnessed to his wagon and the boys had a team of oxen with a small brown mare tied to the lead. Each team was pulling a full load of hay. George decided that the Indians were more likely to go after him and his team of horses since horses were of great value to the Indians. George instructed the boys to unhitch the little brown mare and prepare to ride off on horseback in the opposite direction and hide behind the knolls not far away.

In the meantime, George turned his team for home and the warriors began to ride closer. They approached slowly at first, then without warning there came a war whoop and the chase was on. The boys did what their father instructed them to do. They unhitched the mare. Nat told Robert to get on front and he swung on behind. They turned their mare to the small hills and hoped that their plan to hide from the war party would work.

CHAPTER 9

The Attack

George whipped his team of horses into a full gallop, but the braves quickly closed in on him. A volley of arrows rained down on him as he flung himself into a trench-like depression formed in his load of hay from the binding pole used to secure the load. He gave the team of horses their heads (turned them loose) and they were running at full speed toward home.

George carried a six-shot repeating Spencer rifle with him most of the time and he squeezed off his first shot. The bullet hit home and wounded one of the braves, causing some of war party to turn off. All of them but one fell back. This one brave warrior ran his pony up close behind the lumbering wagon out of George's view and sent an arrow at George striking his jugular vein and lodging in the tissue around his collarbone. From that point on George was unable to fire his rifle but the team had almost reached the house.

George threw himself from the speeding wagon, the horses still pulling with all the strength they had left. He tumbled to the ground not far from the front door of the house with one brave still in hot pursuit. The Martin's oldest daughter, sixteen-year-old Hepzibah, bolted from the front door and blasted a shot with a double barrel shotgun. The brave quickly turned away, leaving her father lying on the ground.

Hepzibah and Ann frantically pulled George into the front room of the house. He was tired and wounded with blood running profusely from his neck, but he was safe for now. Ann Martin, who had some training in the medical field, instructed the children to fetch a long hair from a horse tail. She threaded the horse hair through a needle and stitched closed George's jugular wound.

In the meantime, the two boys, Nat and Robert, were still hiding behind the knolls with the little brown mare. They were watching as their father had raced for his life. It seemed their plan had worked. The Indians didn't seem to care where the boys were. But the little mare began to get restless. She had been away from her foal back at the Martin barn most of the day. The boys tried their best but the little brown mare had made up her mind to return to the barn and the boys were unable to stop her. The mare bolted and they were headed to the barn and in their path were nine or ten Indian braves.

The Indians saw the mare coming at them on a dead run and tried to stop the mare and riders from getting close to the homestead. One of the braves cut across in front of the running mare so close that the little mare reached out and bit the Indian pony on the nape of the neck, causing it to stumble and almost throw the brave.

By this time, the boys and the surrounding pack of Indians were all rushing toward the house. A second brave tried to stop the little mare from reaching home by cutting in front of her to block her path. She reached out to try and bite the brave and instead grabbed the horse blanket beneath him in her teeth and pulled it right out from under him. At this point the Indians must have thought they were not going to stop this little mare from her destination and they started to shoot arrows at the boys.

An arrow from the first Indian who was only four to five feet behind struck Nat in the right elbow. Nat instinctively snapped it off from his elbow and flung it at the brave hitting him in the face. This must have infuriated the brave and he shot another arrow that penetrated Nat's back just below his shoulder blade.

The Indians were at such close range that the arrow had plenty of velocity to pass the arrowhead clear through Nat's back, exiting his chest just below his sternum and lodging in Robert's back very close to his vertebrae. The fletching—the feathered end of the arrow—and much of the shaft were still embedded in Nat's torso. The boys were now pinned together by an arrow as they fled on a running horse.

By this time, the little mare was beginning to tire and slow down. Two more arrows struck the boys, one grazing Nat's thigh and entering Robert's hip. A fourth arrow hit home in Robert's right thigh. The boys—now struck with a total of four arrows—were bloody and weak.

Nat later accounted that he felt the feathered shaft of the arrow inside his chest going back and forth with every stride the little mare took. Nat could no longer stand the pain and passed out pulling his brother Robert off the horse with him.

As they fell to the ground, the force of the fall pulled

the arrow pinning the boys together on through Nat's chest. There they lay helpless, Nat unconscious and Robert delirious with multiple wounds and an arrow in each thigh. The little mare went on a few more steps before she stopped, tangled in the rope the boys had used to hang onto. After running all out for most of a mile with two riders, the little mare was exhausted and was easily captured by the Indians less than a quarter mile from her foal and from the Martin house.

Back at the house, George and Ann could hear all the whooping and shouting, so they had slipped outside and stood on top of the root cellar to get a better look, fearing the worst that it might be the boys trying to get home.

Their fears were justified, because in the distance— about a quarter mile away—they could see the little brown mare running for all she was worth and their two boys surrounded by Indian braves. They were tearing across the hills toward home. As the mare ran closer they could see the boys hunched over and then suddenly they fell to the ground. George and Ann were horrified, but there was little they could do. The Indian mob was out of rifle range and they had three other children in the house to protect.

As the boys tumbled to the ground, the braves decided to make sure they were dead and rode their ponies over the motionless bodies, poking at them with bows and spears to see if they could get a response.

Nat was unconscious and Robert was wise enough to play possum. The Indians rode away, convinced they were dead or close enough that they wouldn't survive. If the boys had been adults, the Indians may have dismounted and scalped their victims. But for Sioux warriors it was not honorable to scalp a "papoose" (the young). So they left them bleeding and dying.

After witnessing Nat and Robert's brutal attack, George and Ann turned their attention to saving the rest of the family. Believing that their sons had been killed, they felt there was no choice but to make a run for it. Their destination was Fort Kearney, about 25 to 30 miles away.

They waited until it got dark to leave.

George—with his neck stitched up with hair from a horse's tail—went outside to gather the team of horses that had become tangled in the traces (reins and wagon harnesses) and now straddled a wood pile. It was impossible to untangle them, so he cut the harnesses to free them. One of the horses had been injured by an arrow that had penetrated deep into his side.

CHAPTER 10

Escape to the West

George and Ann gathered up a few supplies and loaded the three children on the backs of the two horses that had pulled George to safety. They took the horse that was injured, because they didn't want to leave him behind.

It was night, but George knew the lay of the land, and so under the cover of darkness the five Martins set out for Fort Kearney. It didn't take long before they realized two braves were following them at a distance. They continued on their journey hoping for no more confrontation.

After a mile or two the injured horse was struggling so badly that George removed the supplies from his back. They left the horse and went on. The braves who were following came upon the injured horse. Seeing the extent of the injury, they put him out of his misery.

Apparently losing interest, the braves turned around and left the Martin family alone. After a few more miles, as luck would have it, the five Martins came upon the camp of a westbound Freighter wagon train. Understanding their desperate situation, the wagon master invited the Martin family inside the circle of wagons.

By this time all the drivers were curious and they sat around the fire as the Martins told them their harrowing story. George and Ann felt so bad about leaving their two boys on the open prairie they begged the wagon master to leave with them at once and go back to find the boys. But the wagon master refused and told the Martins if the boys are dead "we can do no more for them". He did not want to risk being attacked in the dark.

With that answer and no other options, the Martins bedded down for the night.

CHAPTER 11

Lying on the Prairie

As the last glimpse of sunlight showed over the horizon, the two boys lay motionless on the cooling grass. They had been there about an hour when Nathaniel awoke and in a weak voice murmured, "Robert...are you dead?" Robert responded in disbelief, "Nat! Are you alive?"

Thinking the Indians could still be around, Nat replied quietly, "Robert, don't move. Wait until it gets completely dark and we'll try and get back to the ranch."

So they waited until darkness covered the prairie.

Nat tried to stand up, but he was too weak and the pain too intense. The two boys slowly crawled out of the swale they had landed in when falling from their horse. As they neared the top of a small rise, they could see the faint outline of the house.

It was dark. There was no light coming from the cabin windows. Had their whole family, father, mother and three siblings all been killed or taken? They couldn't know. They only knew they were seriously hurt and they were all alone.

With great effort, the two brothers began their crawl home. It took quite some time and the loss of blood caused them to be light-headed and dizzy. They finally reached the horse trough just outside the barn and cupping their hands, began to drink.

Once their raging thirst had been settled, Nat—who at this point was nearly done-in—finished the final few yards and crawled into the barn. Robert, who had weathered the attack with lessor injury, made his way to the house.

Everything in the house had been turned upside down and provisions were scattered everywhere. The coffee pot had been kicked out the door and flattened against the hitch rail. Indians hated the taste of coffee and seemed to take it out on the pot.

Robert returned to the barn. All the animals were gone; the cattle, the little brown mare's foal, and another foal they were nursing as an orphan. Robert gave Nat the report of conditions in the house. "At least," said Robert, "I found no sign of our family, so they either escaped or were taken."

The two boys, alone and abandoned, worked their way to a pile of hay in the barn, covered themselves to hide from any lingering war parties, and fell asleep.

Chapter 12

"I found them, I found them!"

Early the next morning George and Ann were anxious to head back to the east with the help of the wagon master and crew. The Freighter they were with was traveling west, and they naturally did not want to turn back a half days' drive to the east toward the Martin's ranch.

As luck would have it, another Freighter Train was not far away. They were empty and heading east.

Problem solved.

The Martins would join up with the train headed east.

As the freighter wagons and crew headed east along the Nebraska City Cutoff, word soon spread among the Freighter crew of the Martin's encounter with the Indian war party. They all traveled on with heavy hearts, fully expecting to find the boys dead upon the prairie and perhaps even ravaged by coyotes or wolves.

It was almost two o'clock that day—about 20 hours since the attack—when the Martin homestead came into sight. With the wagon train there was a young man named Beck Martin—no relation—and as the ranch came into view he sped ahead straight for the barn to see if any of the horses were still there. To Beck's surprise he spotted the two boys crawling from beneath the hay.

Beck had stayed with the Martin family a time or two

on previous trips and he recognized them immediately. Beck sprinted from the barn waving frantically and yelling, "I found them, I found them!"

The entire wagon train along with the Martin family raced to the barn. Ann couldn't believe her eyes. Although blood-soaked and dirty from crawling a quarter mile to reach the barn, they were alive and talking. The two boys were immediately mobbed by the family.

Ann with her medical background went into action, quickly giving orders to get her some water and clean cloths. Nat was too weak to even sit up by himself so as he was held, Ann cut away his shirt and began to wash away a large clot of blood from his chest.

"Here is the wound!" she exclaimed. Nat whispered to his mom, "That's where it came out." Ann stunned, asked, "This is where it came out? Where did it go in?" Nat said, "My back." The men helped Ann turn the boy so she could get a better look. What she saw was another large clot of blood just under his right shoulder blade.

Ann had done a fair job of keeping her wits, but at the sight of the second clot she realized with great horror that an arrow had passed completely through her son. She asked, "You're saying the arrow passed clear through your chest?" Nat responded, "Yes, and it stuck into Robert's back. We were pinned together." George, who had been attending to Robert, pointed to the wound in his back. Ann broke down and began to cry. She knew that her son would surely go through a slow and painful death. Nat, hearing his mother's cry whispered, "Mother, I'm not dead yet, so let's see what happens."

In checking Nat over a bit closer, George noticed Nat

had a large swollen right elbow. He examined it carefully and discovered a protruding piece of rawhide string— string that was used to secure an arrowhead. He and Ann knew then that the arrowhead was still in the elbow and a fearful mother told her weakening son, "It has to come out."

So George, with the help of two bull whackers from the wagon train, held the arm steady. George grabbed the tip of the arrowhead with a pair of horse shoe pinchers and pulled to remove the object. The pliers slipped, causing Nat great pain, and he again lost consciousness.

A few minutes later, Nat came to and again his father grabbed hold of the arrowhead as the two men held him down. This time he had a better grip and dislodged the stubborn piece of steel. Nat lost consciousness again and would not awake for almost a day.

All the boys' wounds were cleaned and dressed as best they could. Ann did what she could, but she insisted the boys' only chance to live was if they could be taken to see a doctor.

CHAPTER 13

A Hard Trip

The second day after the boys had been found alive, a decision was made to take Nat and Robert to get medical attention. Fort Kearney was the closest at only two days away by wagon but they were not sure if the Fort Doctor would be there. They could send a rider to the Fort but it would take about a day and a half to get there and back with the news. Ann did not think they could wait any longer. They had to decide which way to travel. West to Fort Kearney and take a chance on medical help or East towards Nebraska City.

The Martins were very familiar with Nebraska City because they traveled there many times getting supplies. They knew they could find medical help there. So the decision was made to haul the wounded boys to Nebraska City.

The trip to Nebraska City was 150 miles and would take five to six days. Even with his neck injury, George loaded up a wagon with hay so the boys could lie on the hay to soften the ride. He hitched their only remaining horse and they started on their journey.

They got off to a late start the first day after spending time scrounging through what was left of their supplies. They only made it ten miles that day. Nat had been unconscious most of the day. The second day the boys ached terribly from their wounds and the jostling of riding in the wagon, and were not convinced they should resume their travels, but Ann insisted. They drove hours and hours, only stopping occasionally to give the boys a drink and let the horse rest.

On the third day it was more of the same; the constant swaying and bouncing of the hay wagon was taking its toll. By the end of that day they reached Beaver Crossing, where they found an abandoned burned out cabin and made camp.

The next morning Nat awoke in such pain that he begged his parents to leave him to die. The incredible pain surging through his entire body was more than he could take.

He had lost his will to live.

He told his parents, "Leave me here and take Robert on to Nebraska City. He has a good chance of making it."

George and Ann had to make a tough decision.

Ann was a strong woman physically and mentally and she was the mother of seven children—a mother who was not going to leave one of her sons there to die in order to save the other one. So the family set up camp the best they could in the old burned out cabin.

Even though they were short on supplies, they would make do. Unfortunately for Ann, she would have to make do without her husband.

The next day, George left his family, taking a minimum amount of supplies. Still in some pain from his injuries, he started walking toward home. After a two-day walk, George reached the homestead where he stayed for only a few minutes to get water and any food that was still available. He continued walking to Fort Kearney, some 25 to 30 miles away. It would take him a full day to reach the fort on foot.

Once there he asked for help and a few supplies. He was told by the commanding officer that they were short-handed and they could not help him. The army had been out patrolling and had been in a few skirmishes themselves and were not interested in helping just one family. The fort was also filled with struggling settlers who were afraid for their lives. The personnel at the fort were overwhelmed.

After a couple days of rest and food, George left the fort in disgust and again on foot headed back toward Beaver Crossing where just a few days earlier he had left his family. Twelve days had passed from the time of his departure from his family and his arrival back to the burned out cabin. During that entire time, George did not know if his sons had perished or just what he might find when he got back to them. He was pleasantly surprised to find both the boys on the mend. Nat and Robert were still weak and in considerable pain but nonetheless, they were alive and in better spirits.

Now George and Ann had to decide what to do next.

Except for their faithful horse, all the rest of their livestock was gone. All their supplies back at the homestead were destroyed. They were determined not to give up. After all, they had a good house, corrals and a barn. They had crops and a garden to harvest. They had enough money saved to buy more supplies in Nebraska City.

So the decision was easy. Back to the ranch they would go.

They loaded up the wagon, hitched their only horse and began the three day trip home. Nat and Robert were strong enough to sit on the spring seat this time, but needed help to get in and out of the wagon.

The trip back was painful for the two boys, but they felt they were going to make it now and were anxious to get home.

CHAPTER 14

Restored

After returning to the ranch and taking a few days to recover from the stressful ordeal, George and Ann Martin realized what a miracle it had been that the family—and especially the two boys so severely injured—had survived. It would be almost a year, but Nat completely recovered from the arrow passing through his chest and was able to put in a full day's work on the ranch. Robert—although not wounded as severely as Nat—would have chronic back pain from his wounds for the rest of his life.

A return to normal life was in store for the Martin family for the next two years. But stories of sporadic attacks by the Sioux and Cheyenne were still ongoing up and down the Platte and south on the Republican River. In June 1868, almost four years after the initial attack on the Martin family, they were victimized again. Only this time they were better prepared, and both Robert and Nat had rifles.

A war party swooped in on some horses the Martins had staked out for grazing and got away with three of them. Without hesitation, Nat, Robert and George pursued the small Indian war party, wounding one of them and retrieving the horses. Altogether, the Martin family would endure a total of four conflicts with warring

Native Americans.

Each time they would manage to survive.

And each time they became even more determined to stay.

Addendum

The location of the Martin homestead and the near fatal attack is well marked with a granite monument located at the intersection of Platte River Road (running directly west from Doniphan, Nebraska) and the Alda Road approximately three miles south of Interstate 80.

Two of the Sioux arrows were retrieved from the attack on Nathaniel and Robert Martin and were donated by Nat's daughter to the Hastings Museum where they are on display.

Portrait of George Martin, circa 1860

George Martin was born in 1819 in Soham, England and died April 18, 1883 at the age of 64 at the original homestead staked in 1862. George was considered an entrepreneur and successful farmer and rancher. He is credited with forming the first post office in Hall County, Nebraska and the Martinville Township.

Portrait of Ann Martin, circa 1860

Ann Martin was born in 1818 in Soham, England and died March 28, 1882 at the age of 63. Ann was the mother of seven children, two with husband George Weavers and five with husband George Martin. Both George and Ann Martin are buried at the Cedar View Cemetery north of Doniphan, Nebraska where a prominent marker still stands with their names.

Portrait of Nathaniel Martin as a young man

Henry Nathaniel "Nat" Martin was born on November 22, 1848 in England and died on May 22, 1928 at the age of 79. Nat received his education in Hall County Nebraska and began farming on his own in 1870. He was married in 1873 to Miss Lititia Donald with whom he had two children, Arthur and Viola. Lititia died in 1877 after just four years of marriage. Nathaniel married her sister Sarah Donald in 1879. Nat went on to become a pillar in his community and a very successful cattle feeder, rancher and farmer. In 1911 he moved to Hastings, Nebraska with his wife Sarah. After she passed away he lived with his daughter, Mrs. A.M. Johnson on North Kansas Avenue until his death in 1928. Nat is buried along with his first wife Lititia and second wife Sarah at Cedar View Cemetery next to his parents.

Robert Ower Martin was born on December 17, 1852 in Cleveland, Ohio and died on March 20, 1899 at the age of 47 in Ellsworth, Kansas. He married Elizabeth Nagle in 1879. Robert lived with constant discomfort from his injuries received to his back from the attack he and his brother survived in 1864 and eventually died from complications of spinal meningitis. Robert is buried in Ellsworth, Kansas.

Martin family at Martin Ranch in 1866
Section 13.9.11 Eight miles west of Doniphan, NE

Gravestone of Henry Nathaniel Martin and wife Sarah

*George Martin
grave monument*

References

Adams County Historical Archives, Hastings Museum

Bad Men and Bad Towns by Wayne C. Lee; Caxton Press; First Edition (January 1, 1993)

Captive of the Cheyenne: The Story of Nancy Jane Morton and the Plum Creek Massacre by Russ Czaplewski; Dawson County Historical Society; First edition (1993)

Cedar View Cemetery, Doniphan, Nebraska

Early Indigenous Indians; Indians.org

Great Platte River Road by Merrill S. Mattes; University of Nebraska Press; Revised edition (November 1, 1987)

Hall County Historical Archives, Stuhr Museum

Hastings Tribune Archives; October 20, 1921

History of Nebraska by James C. Olson; University of Nebraska Press; Second edition (January 1966)

Lincoln Journal-Star; Oregon Trail Cut-Off by Jim McKee

Nebraska Historical Markers

Nebraska State Historical Society

Trade West Publication; Volume 1, Publication 44

Wikipedia – Great Platte River Road; The Oregon Trail; The Mormon Trail; The Homestead Act; The Great Plains

CPSIA information can be obtained
at www.ICGtesting.com
Printed in the USA
FFHW020618220219
50614485-55996FF